CONTENTS

PART ONE: INTRODUCTION TO THE PROPHETIC	8
PART TWO: DIMENSIONS OF THE PROPHETIC MINISTRY	13
PART THREE: 10 ROADBLOCKS OF PROPHETIC ACCURACY	20
PART FOUR: 13 KEYS TO RECEIVE AND RELEASE A PROPHETIC WORD	29
PART FIVE: ACTIVATION AND IMPARTATION	36
CONCLUSION	42
ABOUT THE AUTHOR	44

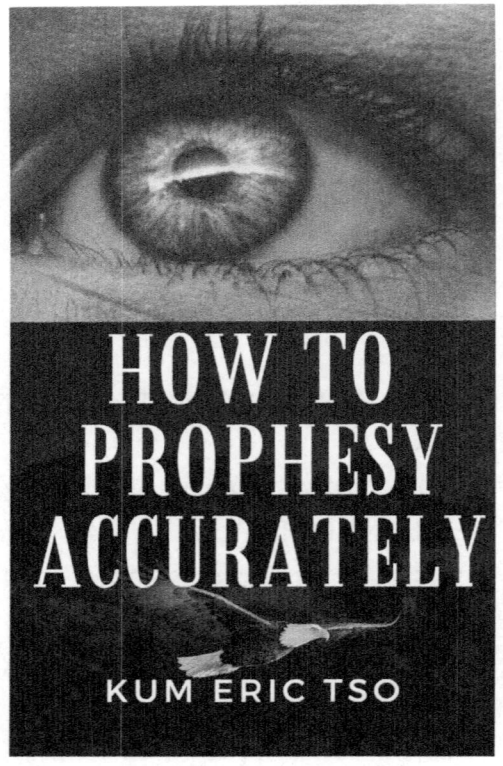

HOW TO PROPHESY ACCURATELY:
13 KEYS TO RECEIVE AND RELEASE A PROPHETIC WORD

KUM ERIC TSO

Copyright © 2022
Kum Eric Tso

Warning

All rights reserved. This is protected under International Copyright Law. No Part of this book may be reproduced, stored in a retrieval system, or transmitted in any form or by any means, electronic, mechanized, photocopy, recording or otherwise without the prior permission of the author in writing.

All biblical quotations used in this book are taken from the New King James Version (NKJV)

Cover Design: Netkipedia

Connect with Author
Website: www.kumerictso.com

E-mail: info@kumerictso.com
Tel: +237 677 44 63 47 (For calls and WhatsApp)

This and other books by Kum Eric Tso are also available at eBook retailers like Amazon

DEDICATION

To all the fathers of the prophetic movement.

"Bless you beloved! I'm Kum Eric Tso, founder of Voice of Dominion Ministries International and today I'll walk you through everything you need to know about prophecy. I pray your understanding of the prophetic grows even as you fulfill your prophetic destiny in the matchless Name of Jesus." Kum Eric Tso

PART ONE: INTRODUCTION TO THE PROPHETIC

Before we see How to prophesy accurately (13 Keys to Receive and Release a Prophetic Word), I want us to, first of all, understand what is prophecy and how the prophets of old or old testament believers received prophetic utterances. I trust this teaching will launch you into a deeper phase in the prophetic. You will learn how to receive and release prophetic utterances effectively.

This kind of teaching and more can be found

on **propheticbibleschool.com**; so, don't forget to **subscribe** for more in-depth teachings.

What Is Prophecy?

The Bible's answer

A prophecy is a message inspired by God, a divine revelation. The Bible says that prophets "spoke from God as they were moved by the Holy Spirit." (**2 Peter 1: 20, 21**) So a prophet is one who receives God's message and transmits it to others. —**Acts 3: 18**.

How did prophets receive information from God?

God used several methods to transmit his thoughts to his prophets:

Writing. God used this method in at least one case by directly supplying to Moses the Ten Commandments in written form. —**Exodus 31:18**.

Oral communication through angels. For example, God used an angel to instruct Moses about the message he was to deliver to Pharaoh of Egypt. (**Exodus 3: 2-4, 10**) When precise wording was crucial, God directed angels to dictate his message, as he did when he told Moses: "Write down these words, because in accordance with these words, I am making a covenant with you and with Israel." —**Exodus 34:27.** *

Visions. These were sometimes given while the prophet was awake and fully conscious. (**Isaiah 1:1; Habakkuk 1:1**) Some were so vivid that the recipient participated in them. (**Luke 9: 28- 36; Revelation 1: 10- 17**) At other times, visions were conveyed while the recipient was in a trance. (**Acts 10:10, 11; 22:17- 21**) God also transmitted his message by dreams while the prophet slept. —**Daniel 7:1; Acts 16: 9, 10**.

Mental guidance. God guided the thoughts of his prophets to convey his message. This is the sense of the Bible's statement: "All Scripture is inspired of God." The phrase "inspired of God" can also be rendered "God-breathed." (**2 Timothy 3: 16**; *The Emphasised Bible*) God used his holy spirit, or active force, to "breathe" his ideas into the minds of his servants. The message was God's, but the prophet selected the wording. —**2 Samuel 23: 1, 2**.

Does prophecy always involve foretelling the future?

No, Bible prophecy is not limited to foretelling the future. However, most messages from God relate to the future, even if only indirectly. For example, God's prophets repeatedly warned the ancient Israelites about their evil ways. Those warnings described the future blessings if the people would heed the warning, as well as the future calamity if they refused. (**Jeremiah 25: 4-6**) The actual outcome depended on the course that the Israelites chose to follow. —**Deuteronomy 30:19, 20**.

Examples of Bible prophecies not involving

predictions

On one occasion when the Israelites asked God for help, he sent a prophet to explain that because they had refused to obey God's commands, He had not helped them. —Judges 6: 6- 10.

When **Jesus spoke to a Samaritan woman**, he revealed things about her past that he could have known only by divine revelation. She recognized him as a prophet even though he had made no **predictions about the future.** — John 4: 17- 19.

At **Jesus' trial**, his enemies covered his face, hit him, and then said: "Prophesy! Who is it that struck you?" They were not calling for Jesus to foretell the future but for him to identify by divine power who had hit him. — Luke 22:63, 64.

PART TWO: DIMENSIONS OF THE PROPHETIC MINISTRY

The prophetic ministry moves beyond just prophesying. It is a lifestyle of bringing God to man and carrying man to God. Helping man to understand who God is, and helping him to walk the way God wants him to walk. The ministry that has the ability to communicate what you have seen and heard. Ability to represent God in every dimension.

DISCERNING OF SPIRIT

It helps us enter into the spirit realm to know the spirit behind any act, to determine whether it is of God or not.

THE SPIRIT OF PROPHECY

The spirit of prophecy is the simplest level of prophetic ministry. It is not a gift. It is not an office. It is an anointing arising from Christ within the believer. It manifests when there is a special prophetic anointing in an area, service or place. Because it is a spirit, it comes and goes. The person is not in possession of the spirit. God uses who you are, what you are to do what He wants to do.

Revelation 19:10

And I fell at his feet to worship him. And he said unto me, See thou do it not: I am thy fellow servant, and of thy brethren that have the testimony of Jesus: worship God: for the testimony of Jesus is the spirit of prophecy.

Believers become channels through which the voice of Christ testifies. When you come into contact with the spirit of prophecy, you have the ability to see and hear in the spirit and operate as a prophet. It also occurs when one comes amongst the company of prophets or the mantle of an anointed prophet is present in a geographical location.

THE GIFT OF PROPHECY

It is the supernatural manifestation of the mind of God by the inspiration of the Holy Spirit and not the human mind. It is not an office, it is a gift. It moves higher than the spirit of prophecy. The gift is subject to the recipient of the gift.

Speaking forth words of the Holy Spirit through an individual to another individual or body of Christ. Special ability given to the believer to receive and communicate timely divine inspired messages from God . it is often the vehicle for the operation of other gifts. It is not for foretelling the future and not predictive by nature.

It has no revelation in it. When it becomes predictive then it means it has blended with the word of wisdom or word of knowledge. Its purpose is limited to edification, exhortation, and comfort. Any believer can operate in the gift of prophecy. Any spirit-filled believer can prophesy but does not necessarily make one a prophet.

Acts 21 : 9

He had four unmarried daughters who prophesied.

THE PROPHETIC GRACE

Romans 12:6

Having then gifts differing according to the grace that is given to us, let us use them: if prophecy, let us prophesy in proportion to our faith;

There are gifts but gifts differ according to the grace. You prophesy according to your faith. It takes great faith to prophesy. It is an unction of the Holy Spirit that gives access into the plans and will of God. An individual with a prophetic grace prophesy frequently, but not with the same level of influence, authority, and power as compared to those called into the office of the prophet. Standing in the office of the prophet goes beyond just seeing and hearing.

The ability to interpret what he is seeing. An example is the sons of the prophet. Sons of the prophet are not yet prophets. Prophets are spiritual military men. Believers with prophetic grace are people who receive dreams, visions, and impressions consistently.

The grace of prophecy is usually in the lives of fruitful ministers. Those with the anointing will exercise prophetic anointing in addition to their specific offices. Their prophecy carries more authority, power, depth, and clarity than someone who operates with the gift of prophecy only.

THE OFFICE OF THE PROPHET

Prophets are not made, trained, they are called by God. You don't desire to become a prophet. You can desire to operate with the prophetic unction. When God calls a man into the office of the prophet, He equips him to operate in that office.

Prophets don't operate with the gift of the spirit, they operate with the gift of the prophet. A nurse is not a medical doctor. This office is not a gift of the spirit. It is an extension of Jesus government over His church. Prophets are trained by God via disappointments, trial. They are dead people. If you are too alive, you cannot be a prophet.

This office touches on areas such as guidance, instruction, rebuke, judgment, and revelation. The office of the prophet is calling from God. The prophet is the custodian of divine secret and the mouthpiece of God, who speaks with divine inspiration. The prophet has the responsibility to equip the saints to discern God's voice and understand His plans and purpose individually and corporately.

No father speaks to his children to another man. Whatever you give attention to grows.

PART THREE: 10 ROADBLOCKS OF PROPHETIC ACCURACY

Woe to them! For they have gone in the way of Cain, have run greedily in the error of Balaam for profit, and perished in the rebellion of Korah. —Jude 11, (NKJV)

Accuracy is important to the prophet's ministry. Accuracy is defined as the quality or state of being correct or precise. There are things that can hinder and block accuracy, such as prejudices, misconceptions, doctrinal obsessions, sectarian views, bitterness, rejection, and lust. Prophets and prophetic people need to be careful that we guard our hearts against things that can block our prophetic flow and the accuracy of the word of the Lord.

Can the fig tree, my brethren, bear olive berries? either a vine, figs? so can no fountain both yield salt water and fresh. —James 3:12

Accuracy is important, and we want to speak what the Father gives us to speak. James talked about both sweet and bitter water coming from the same fountain. Our wells must be pure. What comes forth must be pure. Our fountains must be pure. We cannot allow ourselves to be hindered and bound by our own issues.

Here are some things that can be roadblocks to prophetic accuracy.

1. Too opinionated—Many prophetic people stumble because they feel that their opinion is God's opinion. God's thoughts are always higher than the thoughts of men. Many times prophets can become narrow-minded and dogmatic about revelations they believe to be a truth received from God.

2. Prejudices—This can be cultural or religious. This includes being prejudiced to a race, gender, age group, denomination, or movement.

3. Rejection and fear of rejection—Rejected people need deliverance or they will minister out of hurt. The priests could not have scabs (Lev. 21:20). Scabs are unhealed wounds that can become infected. Rejection leads to isolation, and prophets are called to associate and minister to people. Rejection can lead to prostituting the prophetic gift —prophets giving prophetic words to people just to be accepted by them. The root of this spirit is insecurity. Basically, we reason with ourselves, saying, "I will get acceptance if I tell them what they want to hear." This also leads to flattery.

4. Fear of man—The Bible says, "The fear of man brings a snare" (Prov. 29:25, NKJV). "Snare" is the Greek *mowqesh*, which means to bait, lure. It's an iron ring placed in the nostril of a beast. Fear of man leads us around like a beast with a ring in our nose. We must fear God more than man. The only way to overcome fear is to have faith in God.

5. Bitterness—Unresolved hurts lead to bitterness. Angry and bitter prophets can be tainted in their prophetic flow. Hebrews 12:15 says, "Looking carefully lest anyone fall short of the grace of God; lest any root of bitterness springing up cause trouble, and by this many become defiled" (NJKY). Bitterness can be a root hidden in the heart going undetected. This heart condition springs up at the most inopportune time.

6. Respect of persons—This can be a religious spirit. The high priest carried the stones of all the tribes on his heart, and we should carry

PART THREE: 10 ROADBLOCK...

the whole church in our hearts and not be limited to organizations and denominations. True prophetic ministry will learn how to minister the word of the Lord to all kinds of people and denominations because Jesus is Lord of all the earth. God likes variety and different tribes; that is why He had twelve of them. A Baptist preacher once told me, "I'm Baptist born and Baptist bred, and when I die I'll be Baptist dead." Some people will never leave the church denomination, and this shouldn't disqualify them from receiving a prophetic word.

The prophetic anointing is not designed to change church culture; it's designed to change the hearts and minds of the people who affect the culture. God loves the Baptists. He even had one in the New Testament—John the Baptist. Prophecy is never used to establish new principles in a denomination or organization. A skilled prophetic minister can deliver the heart of God without partiality. I found that many different denomination leaders have invited me to teach and train their people in the prophetic because of trust and relationship. James 2:9 says, "But if ye have respect to persons, ye commit sin, and are convinced of the law as transgressors."

7. Human compassion—This is having compassion on that which God is judging. Jesus rebuked Peter and said, "Get thee behind me, Satan" (Matt. 16:23). Jesus spoke what He saw the Father doing. Prophets cannot allow human compassion to dictate their prophetic flow. There are times you need to minister correction to people you love, and it can be hard, but prophets must pledge their allegiance to the Lamb of God.

Prophesying truth brings deliverance to the hearer. I have learned that every time I neglect to speak the truth to someone, I lose my power to discern or my hearing in that situation becomes dull.

8. Judgmental—This is the opposite of mercy, and when one has a religious spirit he can point out problems with great accuracy but seldom have a solution. All they have done is judged and torn down. Beware of pride and being overcritical. The critical prophet with the pointing of the finger is not ministering out of the heart of God.

9. Judging by appearance—Looking at a person's hand for a ring before giving a word about marriage or looking at someone's countenance for some emotional signals is judging by appearance. Samuel had to anoint David although he was a boy. God told the prophet to judge not according to appearance (1 Sam. 16:7).

10. Lust—The simple definition of lust is having a self-absorbed desire for an object, person, or experience. When we are in lust, we place the object of our desire above all. Prophets must guard their hearts from the lust for power, prestige, promotion, and wealth.

Lust in these areas will cause you to be drawn away from the will of God into a place of error and deception. Unresolved lust issues of the heart have serious implications to the validity of a prophet's ministry. These lust issues create stumbling blocks to accurate prophetic ministry. If you're not delivered from them, they can entice and drag you down a path of falsehood, causing you to potentially become a false prophet. "But every man is tempted, when he is drawn away of his own lust, and enticed" (James 1:14).

Being developed in a sectarian environment is not the best for a prophet. It can warrant any of these issues to taint or color the way a prophet delivers the word of the Lord. Prophets have to be developed in the proper environment, else they can develop or be influenced by religious spirits. Religious spirits are real, and they can work in the environment of churches and sectarian groups.

Religious spirits work where people believe in prophecy and the gifts of the Spirit. We need discernment and deliverance to avoid contamination.

Prophets cannot allow any bias to affect their words. Bias is prejudice in favor of or against one thing, person, or group compared with another, usually in a way considered to be unfair. God is fair, and He is no respecter of persons.

PART FOUR: 13 KEYS TO RECEIVE AND RELEASE A PROPHETIC WORD

Eli taught Samuel how to discern, respond and become sensitive to the voice of God. Prophets can only teach you how to cooperate with the activity of the Spirit, not how to manufacture the Holy Spirit's activity.

1. Put on your priestly garments.

The priestly dimension must return to prophetic people. Prophetic people must put on their priestly garments and spend quality time in the presence of God, understanding their responsibility to minister to God and then to His people. Worshipping God for the testimony of Jesus is the spirit of prophecy. Worship is the doorway to receiving the revelation from God. The apostle John paints a prophetic picture of the lifestyle of a prophetic minister (John 21:20). This verse shows how we must lay our head on the breast of Jesus and listen to the rhythm of His heartbeat being filled with the breath of God. We, in turn, breathe onto others the breath and life received from encountering the Creator. We must develop a relationship and fellowship with the God who knows everything about everything.

2. All of the Lord's words, no matter in what form we hear them, must be quickened and

revealed by the Holy Spirit. *Quicken* means "adding life to ordinary words." The Greek word for *quicken* means "to make alive and give life by spiritual power to arouse and invigorate." The word Jesus speaks has life and vitality. Other words are just dead language. The message can come in a variety of ways—flashes of pictures, Scripture verses, sentence fragments or impressions.

3. Activate faith to operate in the gift of prophecy much as you activated your faith to receive the gift of salvation. You prophesy according to the portion of your faith. The word *proportion* refers to a ratio. You can have faith to prophesy to one person or faith to prophesy to 100 people. It's all based on the proportion of your faith. The apostle Paul challenged Timothy to stir up (rekindle and arouse from dormancy) the gift that was given to him (2 Tim. 1:6).

4. Ask, seek, and knock (Matt. 7:7–11). We can ask God for a prophetic word. Many are afraid

to initiate conversation with the heavenly Father because of fear of deception or demonic interference.

Notice Jesus states that if you ask the Father for gifts, He will not give you something contrary to what you ask. God our Father, who is so in love with human beings, loves to hear the sound of a human voice asking and inquiring of Him. Jeremiah 33:3 says, "Call to Me, and I will answer you, and show you great and mighty things, which you do not know." *Mighty* comes from the Greek word *batsar*, which means "secrets, mysteries, inaccessible things."

5. God will immediately speak something to bless the body. God's first command was to bring light to chaos (Gen. 1:3). God speaks as a means to bring life and order. Since the moon and sun were not created until the fourth day, the light is the presence of illumination in general. Prophetic ministers should speak the light to every dark situation.

6. Focus is the key. Look in the spirit. Ask yourself, "What do I see, feel or have a knowing about the situation?" God speaks through your spirit. It sounds like you. (See Isaiah 21:3–4.)

7. God will quicken one sentence, word, picture or thought to your spirit. Then you must exercise your faith to release the revelation given. It is like a piece of string on a sweater. Give it one pull, and let the words flow. Open your mouth wide, and God will fill it (Ps. 81:10). The Holy Spirit will not move your mouth or override your will. You must give voice to what He is speaking.

8. The manifestation of the spirit is given to every man. *Manifestation* means "to see and behold, to gaze by voluntary observation." It is to inspect, to appear, to discern, to clearly see, to experience, to perceive, to uncover, to lay bare, to reveal. It is also to open to sight, signifying shining. (See 1 Corinthians 12:7.)

9. The end result of prophecy is to find a way to put honor and glory back on mankind and restore what we lost in the garden: relationship to the Father. Everyone wants his or her crown of glory and honor. People are made for validation, celebration, and appreciation.

"What is man that You are mindful of him, and the son of [earthborn] man that You care for him? Yet You have made him but a little lower than God [or heavenly beings], and You have crowned him with glory and honor" (Ps. 8:4–5, AMP).

10. Prophecy releases the power of God, but don't let that be the center of attention. The focus is the heart of God being rightly communicated (1 Sam. 2:35).

11. God will give you a signal in your spirit to what He is about to do. I call them *feelers*. You will know when to look, listen and release.

12. God does not just manifest words; He manifests Himself, so do not quench your emotions. Recognize His thoughts in your mind. We must focus. We have the mind of Christ (1 Cor. 2:16).

13. Recognize the voice of the Lord. God drops things into your spirit, and they manifest on the screen of the spirit called the imagination. Because the Lord speaks through your human spirit, the voice sounds like your voice. It's not normally an outside voice, but the Lord will quicken words to your human spirit, and the voice sounds like you. God speaks through your personality.

God will add life to ordinary words, experiences, and things that you can relate to. Jesus said, "It is the spirit that quickeneth; the flesh profiteth nothing: the words that I speak unto you, they are spirit, and they are life" (John 6:63). Words that are given by the Holy Spirit give life to what would otherwise be dead language.

PART FIVE: ACTIVATION AND IMPARTATION

Many have got the prophetic but are not operating in it because they need an activation. Though they've got the unction, calling or gift, it remains dormant in them. Likewise, others who desire to prophesy accurately simply need a spiritual impartation in order to operate effectively in the prophetic.

How can you activate the prophetic in you?

#1: Know the kind of prophet or prophetic person you are

You need to recognize the gift in you. Recognition enables proper functioning. This is so important since different prophetic dimensions have different purposes. Myles Munroe puts it this way: "When purpose is not known abuse is inevitable." Many are inaccurate because they're trying to function in dimensions in which they're not called.

There are three dimensions of prophets or prophetic people.

a) **Born prophets.** These are those who were foreordained by God as prophets before they were born. This was the case with Jeremiah. *"Before I formed thee in the belly I knew thee; and before thou camest forth out of the womb I sanctified thee, and I ordained thee a prophet unto the nations."* Jeremiah 1:5.

b) **Called prophets.** These are those who are called. That is, you were not born a prophet, neither did you do anything to be one but the executive team in heaven just had a sort of emergency meeting and elected you by grace. This was the case with Amos. *"Then answered Amos, and said to Amaziah, I was no prophet, neither was I a prophet's son; but I was an herdman, and a gatherer of sycomore fruit:"* Amos 7:14.

c) **Made prophets.** I called these ones **made prophets** or **imparted prophets** because they're made prophets not by foreordination nor by calling but by sonship or association. Now, don't mistake these with self-proclaimed prophets. Note that all three types are distinctively expressed in Amos 7:14. Think of the likes of Aaron, Elisha, Joshua who were made prophets as a result of their association with their mentors who were either born or called prophets.

#2: Desire

Paul says in 1 Corinthians 14:1 that we should desire to prophesy. Nothing births and grows the prophetic like desire. Desire unlocks the prophetic realm. Remember the Holy Spirit will never force Himself on you. He is a gentle Spirit. The stronger your desire, the stronger the unction will be.

#3: Have the right motives

You need to have the right motives in order to operate in the prophetic. The prophetic is not given to make you popular, show off, puff up, impress men and all what not. The prophetic is there to help you communicate the heart of God to men.

"Ye ask, and receive not, because ye ask amiss, that ye may consume it upon your lusts." James 4:3

#4: Associate with those in the prophetic.

One of the best ways to unlock the prophetic in you is to associate with those who are already operating in a higher dimension. This can be done in diverse ways. Elisha served Elijah and pursued him diligently in quest for the prophetic gift that was upon his mentor.

PART FIVE: ACTIVATION AND...

Note that you must not necessarily associate with people physically since the association is not even physical but spiritual.

I believe the deepest impartation is not through laying on of hands but through receiving a prophet's teachings and praying together in agreement with a prophet. I currently run an online **Prophetic Bible School** where ministers and believers can connect from across the world and get impacted to fulfill their prophetic destinies. You can join **HERE**.

Amazing testimonies happen as we pray for our students, partners and mentees daily.

#5: Sow into the prophetic anointing

The shortest cut to receive a prophetic impartation is to sow into the prophetic. Let me simply put it this way: when you promote or support what you love, you attract it in your life. You can give into a prophetic ministry or into the life of a prophetic minister as you're led in your heart by the Spirit of God. I won't dwell on this but this really changed my life.

CONCLUSION

In closing, I trust you were richly blessed by this piece and your life shall never remain the same again. My team and I are praying for readers like you to help you fulfill your glorious destiny. Please, feel free to contact me via the following contact information to share your experience, receive an impartation, counseling, or prayer. I will be happy to be the vessel used by God to activate the prophetic in your life.

You could also support us financially to be part of what God is doing through us by reaching out to us by email: **info@propheticbible.com** or by call or WhatsApp through +237 677 44 63 47. This will help us reach out to the untold with the Good News of our Lord and Savior Jesus Christ.

ABOUT THE AUTHOR

Kum Eric Tso is a preacher, entrepreneur, motivational speaker, and author of several best-selling books including **How to Prophesy Accurately: 13 Keys to receive and release a prophetic word**; **How to Recognize The Ideal Man**, and others. He has worked with many church organizations in leadership, and ministry training, church growth, and evangelism. He started evangelizing for Christ at the age of 12 after encountering Christ in the Bible club in secondary school. He will go to the streets of Tiko, a small town in the South West region of Cameroon, and preach the Gospel of Christ at that tender age whilst in secondary school.

The zeal for evangelism kept growing in him even as his prophetic gift started manifesting. He's happily married to Larisa Tso.

For mentorship visit: www.propheticbibleschool.com

Printed in Great Britain
by Amazon